the

LOCOMOTIVE

(its esthetics)

THE NEW VISION

1 AIRCRAFT
BY LE CORBUSIER

2 THE LOCOMOTIVE
BY RAYMOND LOEWY

THE LOCOMOTIVE

BY RAYMOND LOEWY .

Published by Trefoil Publications Ltd, London

ACKNOWLEDGMENTS

THANKS ARE DUE TO THE FOLLOWING SOURCES FOR THEIR COURTEOUS CO-OPERATION

ALSO FOR THE USE OF ILLUSTRATIONS REPRODUCED IN THIS BOOK

Aktuelle Bilder-zentrale, Berlin : 37

Atcheson, Topeka and Santa Fé Railroad, U.S.A. : 50, 119

Austro-Daimler, Austria : 87, 88

Baltimore and Ohio Railroad U.S.A. : 11, 54

Brown : 4, 10

Canadian National Railways : 29, 31 32, 33

Canadian Pacific Railway : 30

Chemins de Fer de L'Etat, France : 36, 94, 95, 96 97, 98

Chemins de Fer Paris-Orléans : 35

Chicago Burlington & Quincy Railroad : 85, 118

County Museum, Truro, Cornwall : 1

Danish State Railways : 92

Delaware and Hudson Railroad, U.S.A. : 47, 48, 49, 51, 53

Dollfus, Charles, Paris : 6, 7

Dmitri, Ivan, New York : 55, 56, 57, 58, 59, 60, 61, 64, 67 74, 78, 79, 103, 104, 105, 106, 107, 114, 115

Fox Photos, Ltd., London : 13, 15, 24, 27

German State Railways : 99, 100

Gidey, H. Gordon : 12

G.P.O. Film Unit, London : 25, 76

Great Western Railway, England : 90, 91

Gulf, Mobile & Northern Railway U.S.A. : 117

H.M. Stationery Office, London : 25, 76

Hoffmann, Berlin : 38

Hübschmann, London : 26, 86, 121, 122, 123 124, 125

L'Illustration : 9

Japanese Government Railways : 40, 41

Kaufmann & Fabry Co., Chicago, U.S.A. : 62, 112

London & North-Eastern Railway, England : 19. 20, 21, 22

London, Midland & Scottish Railway, England : 23, 84

Nederlandsch Spoorweg Museum, Utrecht : 5

Neuperta, Oslo : 46

Newcomen Society Transactions : 2

New York Central Railroad U.S.A. : 52, 63, 65

New York, New Haven & Hartford Railroad, U.S.A. : 116

Pennsylvania Railroad, U.S.A. : 68, 70, 71, 72, 73, 80, 81, 82, 83, 109, 110, 111

Publiciteit Nederlandsche Spoorwegen, Utrecht : 43, 101

Railway Gazette : 8

Richards, Harper : 66, 77

Science Museum, London : 1, 3

Sims, F. & Co., London : 16

South Manchuria Railway Co. : 44, 45

Southern Pacific Railroad, U.S.A. : 75

Southern Railway, England : 26, 124, 125

Sovfoto, U.S.S.R. : 120

Topical Press Agency, Ltd., London : 14, 17, 28, 93

Union Pacific Railroad, U.S.A. : 102

Werner, Louis, New York : 69

Wide World Photos, The New York Times, N.Y. : 18, 34, 39, 42, 89

Zak-Lownsbery & Associates, U.S.A. : 113

PREFACE

COUNTLESS BOOKS HAVE BEEN WRITTEN ABOUT THE LOCOMOTIVE : ITS HISTORY, ITS SAFETY, ITS ECONOMICS AND ITS ROMANCE — LITERATURE OFTEN AS REMARKABLE AS THE SUBJECT IT COVERS. I FELT THAT THE "NEW VISION SERIES" SHOULD MAKE NO ATTEMPT AT COVERING SUCH GROUND; IT HAS ALREADY BEEN DONE IN A MASTERLY WAY.

MY YOUTH WAS CHARMED BY THE GLAMOUR OF THE LOCOMOTIVE. I AM STILL UNDER ITS SPELL AND IN THIS VOLUME I WOULD RATHER WRITE ABOUT THE BEAUTY OF THE MAGNIFICENT CREATURE TO WHOM I OWE SOME OF MY MOST CHERISHED SOUVENIRS.

UNABLE TO CONTROL AN IRRESISTIBLE CRAVING TO SKETCH AND DREAM LOCOMOTIVES AT THE ODDEST MOMENTS, IT WAS A CONSTANT SOURCE OF TROUBLE DURING MY COLLEGE DAYS, AND THE DESPAIR OF MY PROFESSORS. LATER, AS A YOUNG MAN, IT LED TO MY COMPLETE OBLIVION AS A DANCING PARTNER, FOR I SPENT LONG, ENCHANTING HOURS AT THE LOCOMOTIVE DEPOT INSTEAD OF TAKING SCHEDULED DANCE LESSONS. I HAVE NO REGRETS. IN RECENT YEARS IT HAS BEEN MY PRIVILEGE TO DESIGN ALL SORTS OF THINGS, SUCH AS STREAMLINED SHIPS, TRANS-CONTINENTAL MOTOR BUSES, AUTOMOBILES AND ELECTRIC ENGINES. NEVER DID I DREAM THAT MY CAREER AS AN ARTIST-ENGINEER WOULD LEAD ME SOME DAY TO THAT GLORIOUS ADVENTURE, THE DESIGNING OF A STEAM ENGINE. AND STILL THE DAY HAS ARRIVED. LAST YEAR, ON MARCH THIRD, MY FIRST STREAMLINED LOCOMOTIVE, DEVELOPED IN COLLABORATION WITH THE ENGINEERING DEPARTMENT OF THE PENNSYLVANIA RAILROAD, WAS PLACED IN OPERATION. IT WAS AN EVEN GREATER THRILL THAN I HAD EXPECTED.

TO ENGINE 3768 MY HEARTIEST WISHES FOR A FAST AND BRILLIANT CAREER.

RAYMOND LOEWY

NEW YORK, 1937.

MAJOR TYPES OF LOCOMOTIVES

MOGUL	2-6-0
PRAIRIE	2-6-2
ATLANTIC	4-4-2
TEN WHEELER	4-6-0
PACIFIC	4-6-2
HUDSON	4-6-4
CONSOLIDATION	2-8-0
MIKADO	2-8-2
BALTIC	2-8-4
MOUNTAIN	4-8-2
CONFEDERATION	4-8-4

WITHOUT GOING INTO DETAILS ABOUT THE HISTORY OF THE LOCOMOTIVE, LET US LOOK RAPIDLY AT SOME OF THE EARLY ATTEMPTS AT AUTOMOTION ON RAILS.

1. RICHARD TREVITHICK'S "CATCH ME WHO CAN" (1808).
(From a photograph in the Science Museum, London, of an original in the County Museum, Truro.)

One of the "GIANT OF CORNWALL" early designs and a very good looking one. His first locomotive operated on rails in 1804. Trevithick is undoubtedly the inventor of the locomotive.

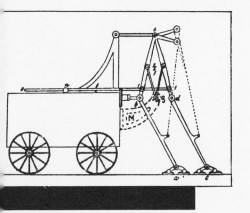

FIGURE I.
Lateral Elevation.

2. Wm. BRUNTON'S "STEAM HORSE" (1813) (Newcomen Society Transactions) used to be propelled by two mechanical legs, functioned for approximately two years, was nicknamed the "GRASS-HOPPER," and finally ended its career in a terrific explosion.

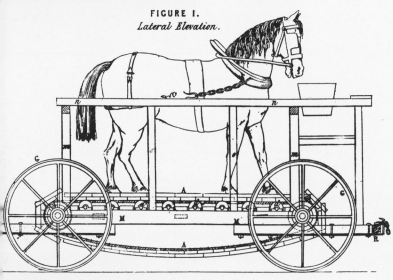

3. BRANDRETH'S "CYCLO-PEDE" (1829). (From a drawing in the Science Museum, London.) One of the first horse propelled vehicles. Notice the water pail in front of the horse.

4. DETMOLE'S FLYING DUTCHMAN (1829). (After Brown.) Detmole's contraption transported 12 passengers at 12 M.P.H. between Charleston and Hamburg (U.S.A.).

5. STEINHEIL'S "HORSE LOCO-
MOTIVE" (1853). (A drawing by
J. A. Maronier after an old repro-
duction. By courtesy of the
Nederlandsch Spoorweg Museum,
Utrecht.) A high-powered cyclo-
pede tested in Berlin in 1853.

6. MEDHURST'S "NEW SYSTEM
OF INLAND CONVEYANCE"
(1827) (Collection M. Charles Dollfus)
was never built, but it led the
way to numerous pneumatically
propelled vehicles. Medhurst,
according to Charles Dollfus, is the
first inventor who specified streamlining in conjunction with moving
vehicles. He wrote that "The
body shall be tapered at both front
and rear ends so the car will move
through still air or head winds
with a minimum of resistance."

7. ANDRAUD'S COM-
PRESSED AIR LOCOMOTIVE
(1839) (Collection Charles M.
Dollfus) and other develop-
ments in the electric propul-
sion field were the direct
result of an epidemic of ex-
plosions of steam locomotives.

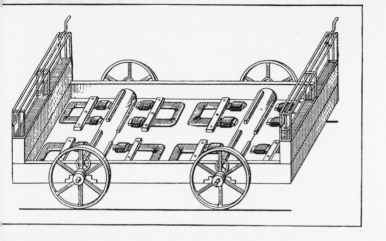

8. ROBERT DAVIDSON'S ELECTRIC LOCOMOTIVE (1842) (Railway Gazette, 1934) went through experimental stages on the Edinburgh and Glasgow Railway. Speed 4 M.P.H.

9. "CANIPOSTE" RAILWAY (1845) (L'Illustration, 1845) was used in Belgium for fast mail transportation. A stuffed hare is fastened at the end of a rod in front of the two hungry dogs. An improved model used a chunk of fresh meat.

10. SOUTH CAROLINA RAILROAD COMPANY'S "SAILCAR" (1829) (After Brown) ran between Charleston and Hamburg, conveying 15 passengers at a maximum speed of 15 M.P.H.

11. THE BALTIMORE AND OHIO'S "PIONEER" (1829) used to operate between Baltimore and Ellicott's Mills, 13 miles distant. Although not a self-propelled unit, this used to travel on rails.
(Photo Courtesy Baltimore & Ohio.)

12. Pre-streamlining days at their best. Beautiful example of clean-cut locomotive engineering. *(Photo H. G. Gidey.)*

GREAT WESTERN'S "KING HENRY VII." Powerful looking, free to a certain extent from projecting units, this is a quite attractive design. It retains the familiar "Locomotive look" that competent streamline engineers will try to preserve as it is not necessarily incompatible with efficient airfoil conformation. (*13. Fox Photos.*)

THE SILVER LINK, rather efficiently streamlined, but somewhat lacking in grace. However, the side elevation shown below has more attractive lines. The tender blends well with the engine as a whole.   (No. 14 Topical Press. No. 15 Fox Photos.)

(Photo F. Sims & Co.)

No. 17 Topical Press.)

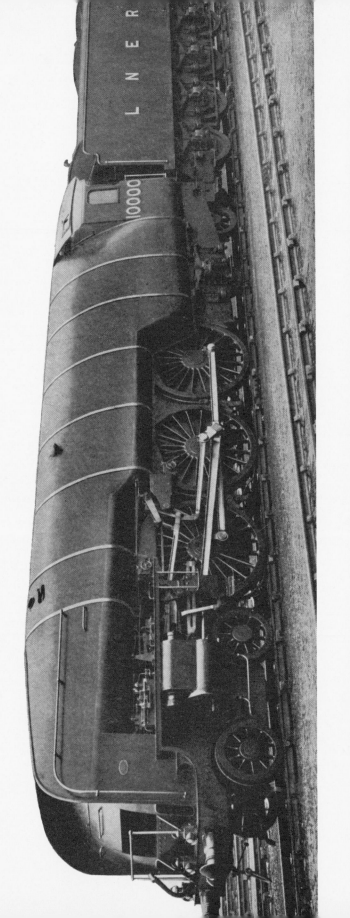

19. The famous L.N.E.R. 10,000. A most important experiment in streamlining and high pressure boiler. Notice attention given to smoke deflector. The entirely concealed smoke stack is disturbing. The out-up appearance is due to a great extent to the bright finish cross sectional bands. Horizontal treatment would have greatly improved this otherwise remarkable Hudson type engine.

(*Photo L.N.E.R.*)

20. L.N.E.R. 10,000

21. This type of tender is used on the non-stop "FLYING SCOTSMAN" to enable the engine crew to be changed during the run. (Photos L.N.E.R.)

22. GARRATT TYPE ENGINE. Powerful looking, but rather unattractive due to lack of homogeneity in design. The two end units do not blend in. This could have been partially achieved.

(Photo L.N.E.R.)

23. L.M.S. TURBINE LOCOMOTIVE. In the writer's opinion, a truly splendid engine, and an outstanding example of the "British School." The cut in the rear top section of the tender might have been omitted, creating a longer horizontal outline. However, it is as a whole one of the most beautiful pieces of machinery ever designed by man. It has the poise, the rhythm and the balance reminiscent of some magnificent ship. This engine probably represents the apex of the pre-streamlined era.

(Photo L.M.S.)

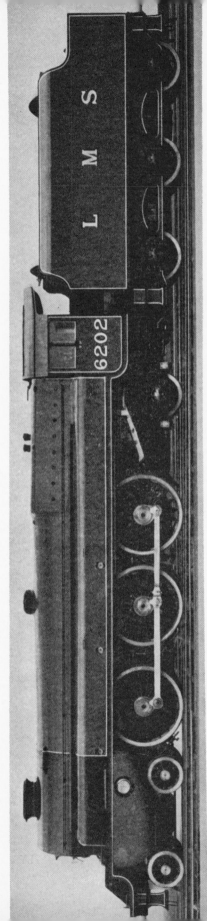

24.   GREAT WESTERN'S "KING HENRY VII."   Engine and tender blend well.   Smoke deflection has not been taken care of, but this engine has aesthetic possibilities.   *(Fox Photos.)*

25.   SILVER JUBILEE IN ACTION.   The captivating beauty of power and speed.   A thoroughbred. *(Courtesy Controller, H.M. Stationery Office and G.P.O. Film Unit.)*

26. Impressive British Classic of the Southern Railway, LORD COLLINGWOOD, with unimpressive smoke deflectors

27. COCK O' THE NORTH on Forth Bridge. Let's hope that the tendency to simplification evident in the engine will some day apply to bridge designs. *(Fox Photos, Ltd.)*

28. GREAT WESTERN'S "SHOOTING STAR" being roller-tested at 85 miles per hour. Accurate data is thus secured in reference to stability, pulling power, and coal and water consumption. *(Photo Topical Press.)*

29. Locomotive of the CANADIAN NATIONAL RAILWAYS being cleaned at Point St. Charles.

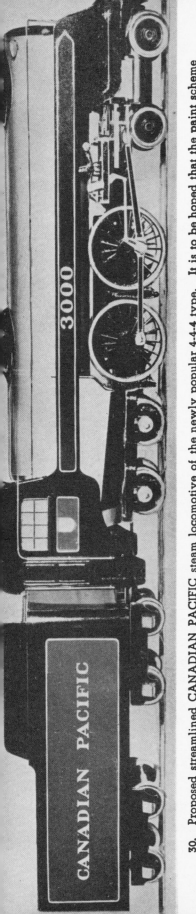

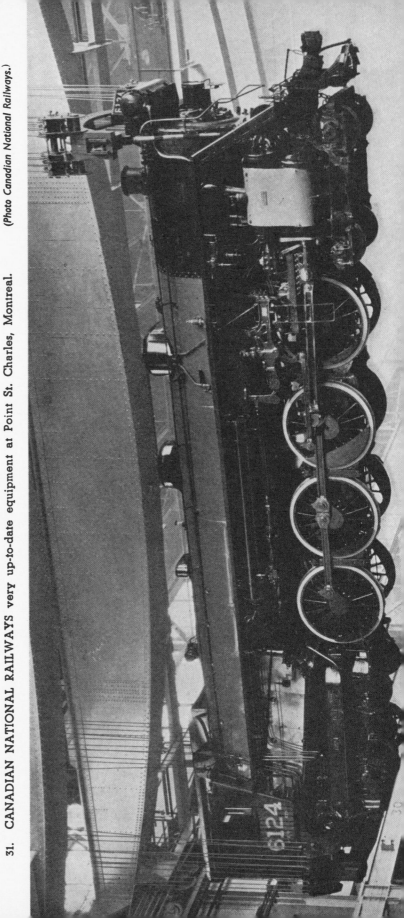

30. Proposed streamlined CANADIAN PACIFIC steam locomotive of the newly popular 4-4-4 type. It is to be hoped that the paint scheme will be revised in order to improve the really inharmonious cut-up appearance of this peculiar vehicle.
(Photo Canadian Pacific Railway.)

31. CANADIAN NATIONAL RAILWAYS very up-to-date equipment at Point St. Charles, Montreal.
(Photo Canadian National Railways.)

32. On "Airstream" engines most of this paraphernalia is concealed by a steel shell. Instantaneous accessibility is required for oiling and maintenance, confronting the designer with one of the major problems in the streamlining of locomotives.   (*Photo Canadian National Railways.*)

A " streamliner's " nightmare !

(33. Photo Canadian National Railways.)

FRANCE

PARIS, LYON, MEDITERRANEE'S new streamlined locomotive. The smoke deflecting device is reminiscent of L.N.E.R. 10,000. Note perfect blend of engine and tender. Visibility from engineer's cab excellent. Streamlining good. (34. *Photo Wide World*.)

35.   An odd looking machine.   P.O. Railways. *(Photo Paris Orleans.)*

36.   STATE RAILWAYS powerful, fast mountain type locomotive.   Several Units on top of the boiler have been faired in one group. A clean arrangement. The smoke deflector adds nothing to the general appearance.   *(Photo Etat.)*

GERMANY

GERMAN STATE RAILWAYS' streamlined engine. Clumsy appearance might conceivably be excused for the sake of streamlining. However, more than 100 tests conducted in 1935 by the author and his assistants in New York University's wind tunnel has proven conclusively that such a shape is not satisfactory from a smoke deflection viewpoint, as it creates low-pressure areas on either side of the engine, dragging smoke down in front of the cab, obscuring windows. (37. *Photo Aktuelle Bilder-zentrale, Berlin.*)

Due to the probable failure of the smoke deflecting device as shown on previous photograph, extra screen plates have been added on either side of the funnel, penalizing the general appearance to a still greater extent. (38. *Photo Wide World.*)

The same engine showing the interesting lower rolling side panels provided for maintenance. The smoke deflecting device seems inadequate. An objectionable feature is the "swept-in" conformation of the lower front end. In case of collision with a vehicle the wreckage may get jammed underneath and de-rail the locomotive. Notice attention paid to this contingency in latest American designs. (39. *Photo Hoffmann, Berlin.*)

JAPAN

JAPAN'S 'STREAMLINER'
relies on four troughs for
smoke lifting, creating a
decidedly complicated
front end and probably a
very turbulent air flow.
*(40. Photo Japanese Government
Railways).*

It will be very interesting,
if not amusing, twenty
years from now, to look
again at streamlining's
early efforts in the railroad
field. *(41. Photo Japanese
Government Railways.)*

NETHERLANDS

Another attempt at streamlining, somewhat similar to America's COMMODORE VANDERBILT. Clean and quite simplified, but somewhat unexciting. The old-fashioned kerosene lamps are decidedly quaint. The tapered shape of the engine tends to create a low pressure area on the lee side, especially in a yaw, thus counteracting the effect of the smoke deflector.   (42. *Photo Wide World.*)

Excellent tie-up between cab and tender: over-slanted cab window may create light reflection problems, poor visibility   All in all a design that will not stand the test of time, even of short time.
(43. *Photo Publiciteit Nederlandsche Spoorwegen.*)

MANCHOUKUO

44. An interesting front end on an engine built as early as 1934. *(Photo South Manchuria Railway Company.)*

Built by the SOUTH MANCHURIA RAIL-
WAY Company workshops and KAWA-
SAKI SHARYO Company, this locomotive
denotes careful study of details. A rather
nice engine. The tender is well worked
out, smoke deflecting scheme inadequate.
(45. *Photo South Manchuria Railway Company.*)

NORWAY

NORWEGIAN STATE RAILWAYS. An impressive engine, partly spoiled like so many others by a set of ineffective and unsightly smoke deflectors. The cylindrical tender is unusual. As a whole, too many superimposed accessories, pipes and rods. (46. *Photo Neuperta, Oslo.*)

DELAWARE & HUDSON'S adaptation
of the roller bearings to the main driving
shaft.   (47.   *Photo Delaware and Hudson.*)

DELAWARE AND HUDSON'S early, but rather unattractive attempt at streamlining. Top heavy, but nevertheless a creditable effort toward the "NEW" locomotive. The surface has been cleaned-up a certain amount. (1930.) (48. Photo Delaware and Hudson.)

Built by DELAWARE AND HUDSON as early as February, 1930, this is indeed a successful attempt at simplification. Strongly influenced by the "British School," this engine presents some of the clean-cut, precise details familiar to English locomotives. Notice partially built-in headlights. A good start toward simplicity. (49. *Photo Delaware and Hudson.*)

ATCHESON, TOPEKA AND SANTA FÉ. Interesting through its mere size, this gigantic twenty-four wheel Mallet Type engine was built in 1913. (50. *Photo Atcheson, Topeka and Santa Fé.*)

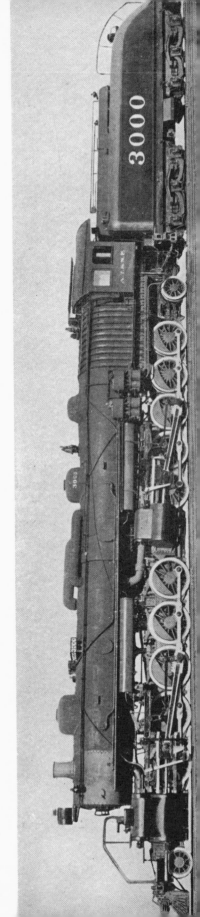

51. WHAT PRICE SMOKE DEFLECTION? The small degree of efficiency of these smoke deflectors does not excuse their spoiling the front end of the engine. (*Photo Delaware and Hudson.*)

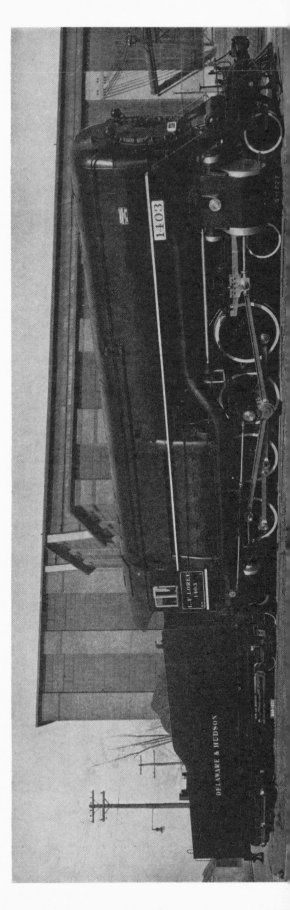

NEW YORK CENTRAL'S MOUNTAIN TYPE LOCOMOTIVE. These tremendously fast, powerful locomotives are of the celebrated Mountain Type. It has the high wheels and speed of the Pacific Type, but its added length gives it the steaming capacity of its ancestors, the slow, lumbering Decapod. This recent locomotive has the new type disc wheels. It is regrettable that an engine of such noble proportions should be buried under a maze of tubes, rods and gadgets. A splendid opportunity lost.

(52. *Photo New York Central.*)

L. F. LOREE (1933). Four cylinder triple expansion locomotive. The complete elimination of smoke stack gives an unfinished appearance to the engine. The huge pipe on the side looks somewhat crude. However it represents an important step toward the future due to its partial elimination of projecting elements. Compare with the engine above.

(53. *Photo Delaware and Hudson.*)

BALTIMORE AND OHIO'S "ROYAL BLUE" (1935).
America's latest type of non-streamlined locomotive,
this engine is neat in appearance and well adapted
to fast, light weight duty. (54. *Photo Baltimore and Ohio.*)

(56. *Photo Ivan Dmitri.*)

Compare the apparent complication of this running gear with the NEW YORK CENTRAL engine below.

A new type of balanced disc wheel greatly contributing to modernized appearance.

(57. Photo Ivan Dmitri.)

"THE OLD VISION" that still gives a heartbeat to lovers of atmosphere and railroad "Romance."   (58. *Photo Ivan Dmitri.*)

59 and 60. NEW YORK CENTRAL before the New Vision,
all the glamour of the Steam Age. (*Photo Ivan Dmitri.*)

61. The Gentleman at the controls. *(Photo Ivan Dmitri.)*

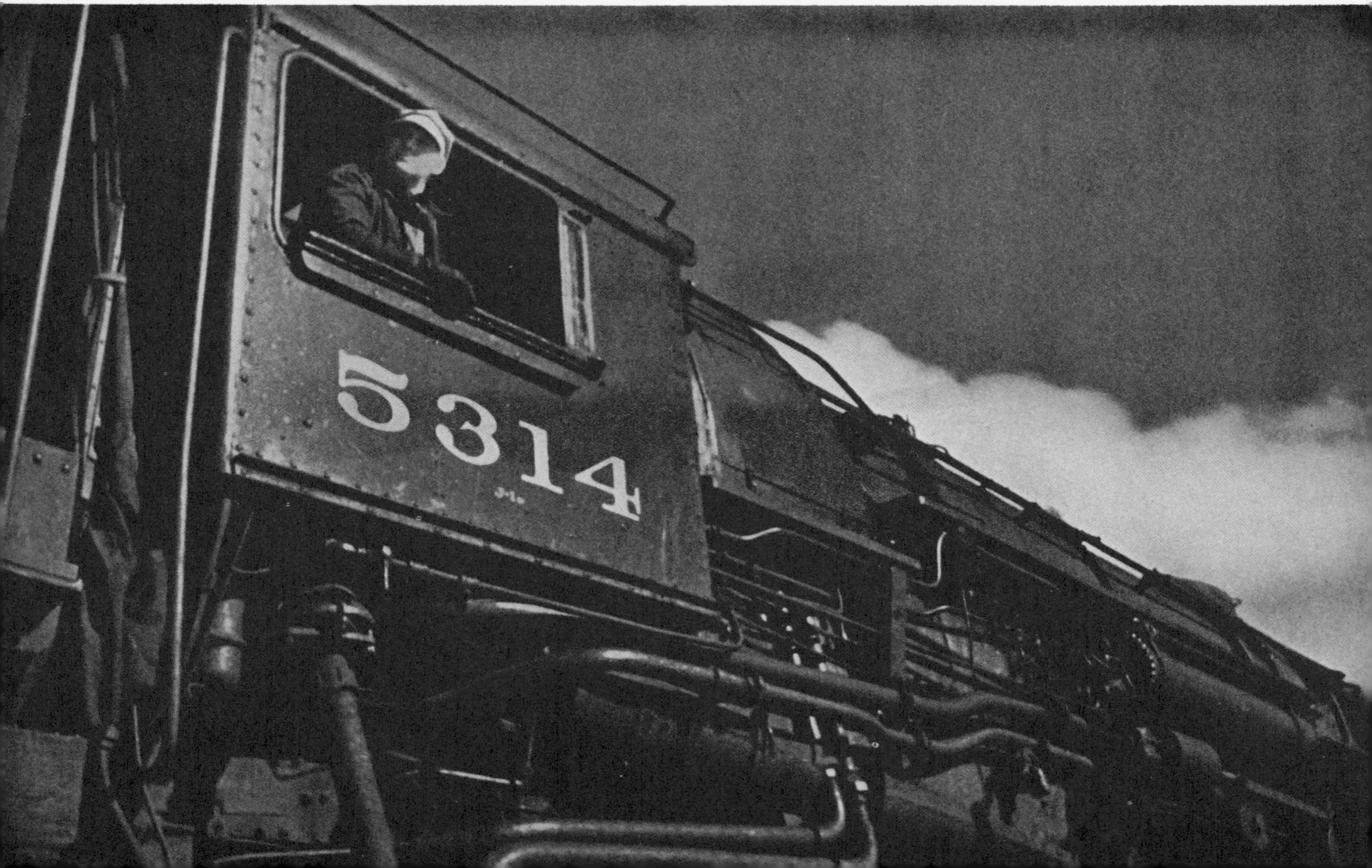

(Photo Kaufmann & Fabry Co.)

62. "HIAWATHA," THE MILWAUKEE ROAD'S
streamliner. A very fast engine intended for
light-weight operation. Entirely jacketed with
stainless steel, it offers a smooth surface, ties up
nicely with the tender, but somewhat lacks the
"steam-locomotive" feel. Its orange and aluminium
colour scheme is rather irritating.

COMMODORE VANDERBILT (1935). NEW YORK CENTRAL'S streamline giant presents a smooth surface. However, it looks like a cover of sheet steel put on as an after-thought over a standard engine. It looks that "typromotion feeling" mentioned before which sentiments a train must derive

(63. Photo New York Central.)

64. THE COMMODORE VANDER-BILT on its way. *(Photo Ivan Dmitri.)*

65. NEW YORK CENTRAL'S MERCURY, 1936 version of the Commodore Vanderbilt. An improvement, no doubt (Photo New York Central.)

PENNSYLVANIA RAILROAD'S streamlined engine (1936). This engine was designed by the author in conjunction with the Engineering Department. More than 100 tests were made in the wind tunnel before the design was adopted. Small clay models were used. At maximum speed a 33% reduction in air resistance was obtained over a similar non-streamlined engine. The smoke deflecting device proved most successful in lifting the smoke over and above the engine and tender, thoroughly vindicating wind tunnel results.

(66. *Photo Harper Richards.*)

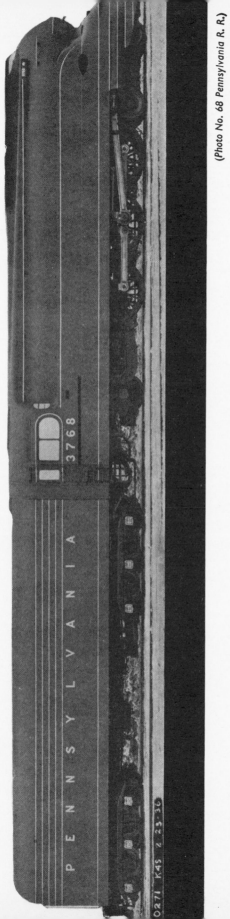

Above, photograph of the actual engine and tender. Below, photograph of the scale clay model used in wind tunnel test. Notice the very close similarity.

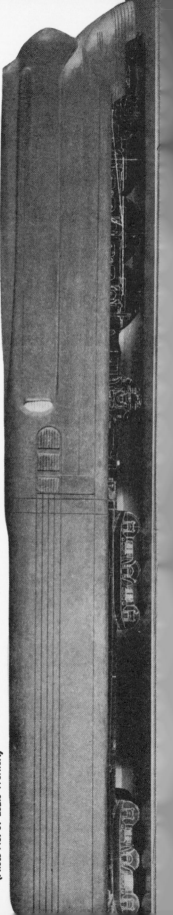

70. The front coupler compartment closed.

71. Opened.

72. The front coupler swung forward into operating position.

73. Side panels are quickly removable for maintenance. *(Photo Pennsylvania Railroad.)*

74. A step toward the
future. (*Photo Ivan Dmitri.*)

SOUTHERN PACIFIC locomotive built for cab forward operation. Tremendously powerful, they haul heavy trains over the Sierra Nevada mountains. *(75. Photo Southern Pacific.)*

EVOLUTION OF THE SMOKE STACK (Photo No. 76 Controller, H.M. Stationery Office and G.P.O Film Unit. Photo No. 77 Harper Richards.)

THE ENGINEER'S CAB of the PENNSYLVANIA'S streamlined engine.   Note absence of all rivets on the surface.

(78.   *Photo Ivan Dmitri.*)

PRESENTATION
TO THE PRES
in Philadelphi
The electric eng
ine next to th
steam locomotiv
was designed b
the author in co
operation with
the Engineerin
Department of th
PENNSYLVANIA
RAILROAD.

(79. *Photo Ivan Dmitr*

80. EVOLUTION OF THE CAB. Cumberland Valley Railroad. *(Photo Pennsylvania Railroad.)*

81. PENNSYLVANIA RAILROAD'S Streamlined Cab. *(Photo Pennsylvania Railroad.)*

EVOLUTION OF THE HEADLIGHT from the "John Bull" to the PENNSYLVANIA RAILROAD'S
streamlined locomotive. *(82 and 83. Photos Pennsylvania Railroad.)*

EVOLUTION

WE HAVE WITNESSED THE
EVOLUTION OF THE STEAM
LOCOMOTIVE AND ITS VIOLENT
PLASTIC TRANSFORMATIONS DUR-
ING THE PAST FIVE YEARS OR SO.

WHAT HAS HAPPENED TO THE DIGNIFIED SUB-LETHARGIC REPOSE OF OUR OLD FRIEND? WHY THIS SUDDEN AWAKENING THAT MAKES TRANSPORTATION HISTORY? IT IS THE LOCOMOTIVE'S ANSWER TO THE APPEARANCE OF A NEW TYPE OF MOTIVE POWER: THE DIESEL-ELECTRIC PLANT.

THIS HIGHLY COMPACT UNIT GAVE BIRTH TO DIFFERENT TYPES OF AUTOMOTIVE EQUIPMENT — STREAMLINED, EFFICIENT, BUILT OF ALUMINIUM ALLOYS AND HIGH TENSILE STEELS. ALTHOUGH THESE SNAPPY LOOKING VEHICLES CAN HARDLY BE CLASSIFIED AS "LOCOMOTIVES," THEY NEVERTHELESS DESERVE OUR CAREFUL ATTENTION BECAUSE OF THE DEFINITE INFLUENCE THEY WILL HAVE ON STEAM LOCOMOTIVE DESIGN. SOME OF THE LATEST ELECTRIC ENGINES MUST BE TAKEN INTO CONSIDERATION FOR THE SAME REASON.

IT WILL BE READILY NOTICED AMONG THE FOLLOWING EXAMPLES OF ELECTRIC AND DIESEL-ELECTRIC VEHICLES THAT UNLIKE THE STEAM LOCOMOTIVE WHICH RETAINS DECIDEDLY "RACIAL" CHARACTERISTICS, THESE NEWCOMERS IN THE RAILROAD WORLD OBEY NO OTHER LAWS THAN WEIGHT AND AERODYNAMICS. GENERALLY SPEAKING, THE DIESEL-ELECTRIC UNITS ARE RATHER CRUDE FROM AN AESTHETIC VIEWPOINT, BUT WE SHOULD NOT BE TOO CRITICAL OF THESE FIRST EFFORTS. THEY CORRESPOND TO AVIATION'S EARLY STRUGGLE TWENTY YEARS AGO. NO DOUBT THEY WILL EVOLVE TOWARD VERY BEAUTIFUL LINES AND BRING ABOUT HIGHER SPEEDS, FOR THEY ARE COMPARATIVELY LIGHT AND KIND TO THE TRACKS

ROADBEDS, THE *REAL* KEY TO HIGHER SPEEDS.

(84. Photo L.M.S.)

THE NEW VISION.   Light weight Diesel power-unit against old-fashioned weight and bulk.

(Photo No. 85 Chicago, Burlington & Quincy Railroad.)   *(Photo No. 86 Hubschmann.)*

AUSTRIA

An example of weight reduction
carried to the extreme   This
almost airplane technique. However
efficient, diagonal structural trusses
are disturbing from an aesthetic
viewpoint. (87. Photo Austro Daimler)

88. THE AUSTRO DAIMLER Railcar, somewhat influenced by the bus, the street car and the airplane. The oilcloth apron is regrettable. (Photo Austro Daimler.)

BRITAIN

89. SPOTLESS MAINTENANCE! A unique feature
of the "British School." (*Photo Wide World.*)

GREAT WESTERN RAILCARS are very interesting. They might be among the very best were
it not for the unhappy treatment of the lower
side walls. Too many doors, panels, grills and
louvres. It is hard to eliminate them, I know,
but it can—and will eventually—be done.
Excellent front-end airfoil formation, but haz-
ardous in case of automobile collision.

(90 and 91. Photo Great Western Railway.)

DENMARK

Not quite so successful as the Netherland's articulated train, this DANISH RAILWAYS' train is nevertheless a credit to its designers.   (92. *Photo Danish State Railways.*)

FRANCE

THE MICHELINE. The operator's cabin affords excellent visibility on a 360° field. The vehicle is rubber tired.

(93. *Photo Topical Press*.)

94. "AUTOMOTRICE" RENAULT. Lacks unity in blending the different units. Not so very attractive as a whole. An unfortunate front end treatment.

95. This **BUGATTI** group has also a turret type control booth. Unsophisticated streamlining, angular edges, poor airfoil.

96. "AUTOMOTRICE" ACIERIES DU NORD. Not so very good as far as airfoils go. *(Photo Etat.)*

"AUTOMOTRICE" SOMUA. Neat design. The undercarriage has been carefully worked out in order to reduce ground drag. (97. Photo Etat.)

'AUTOMOTRICE' RENAULT. About the best so far in France from both aerodynamic treatment and appearance. Quite an achievemen. and symptomatic of rapid progress in design. (98. *Photo Etat.*)

GERMANY

GERMAN STATE RAILWAYS.
A more harmonious window
treatment would improve this
otherwise attractive twin-unit.
(99. Photo German State Railways.)

**GERMAN STATE RAILWAYS
TWIN-UNIT TRAIN.** Windows
are too angular. However,
clean-cut, simple, this is a
grown-up design free from
fancy decorations. Really good.
(100. Photo German State Railways.)

NETHERLANDS

Three cheers for this. In the writer's opinion it is the best looking Diesel-electric unit-train built so far. Its aerodynamics are nearly perfect; the front end treatment and the flush side windows are most attractive and efficient. Paint scheme good. This is an excellent example of what good taste and restraint can produce. (101. *Photo Publiciteit Nederl. Spoorwegen.*)

UNITED STATES

The first Diesel-electric streamliner; built for the UNION PACIFIC by PULLMAN.   Already slightly obsolete front-end treatment, but undoubtedly the pioneer in the field.   As in all American trains, careful attention has been given to collision possibilities.   *(102. Photo Union Pacific.)*

103. Side-
walls are
tapered,
the under-
carriage
curved in.
Good visi-
bility afford-
ed from the
engineer's
cab.
(Photo Dmitri.)

The gap between motorized unit and next car has been covered with a flexible diaphragm, a practice now generally adopted in unit-train construction.

(104. Photo Ivan Dmitri.)

105 and 106. Clean,
efficient re-fuelling.
(*Photo Ivan Dmitri.*)

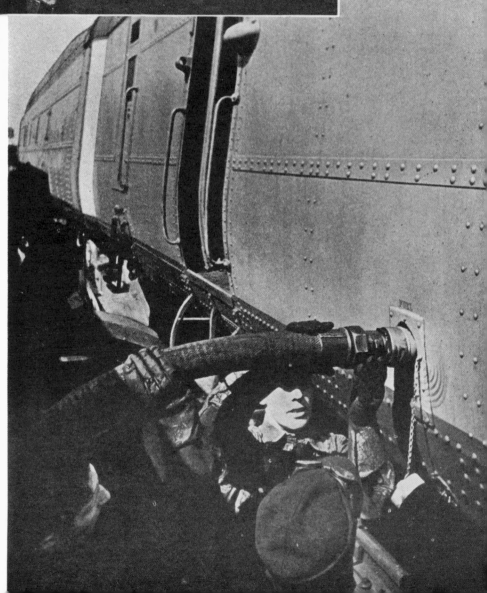

The undercarriage treatment of the UNION PACIFIC unit-train represents an honest effort at streamlining. The unwelcome rivet heads are disturbing. (107. Photo Ivan Dmitri.)

108. PENNSYLVANIA RAILROAD'S ELECTRIC LOCOMOTIVE. 57 of these engines were built in 1935. Ninety feet long, they develop 4,500 H.P. and are capable of a speed of 120 miles an hour. Planned to operate in either direction they have been partially streamlined accordingly. The author acted as consulting designer in the styling of these engines.

Designed in 1935, the PENNSYLVANIA RAILROAD locomotives represent the most up-to-date design in electric motive power. Entirely butt-welded the shell is perfectly smooth and rivets have been eliminated. With the exception of the pantagraphs nearly all projections have been eliminated. Notice faired-in lights.

This illustration gives a fair idea of the relative dimensions of these giant electric locomotives compared with the steam engine in the foreground.

(109 and 110.   Photos Pennsylvania Railroad.)

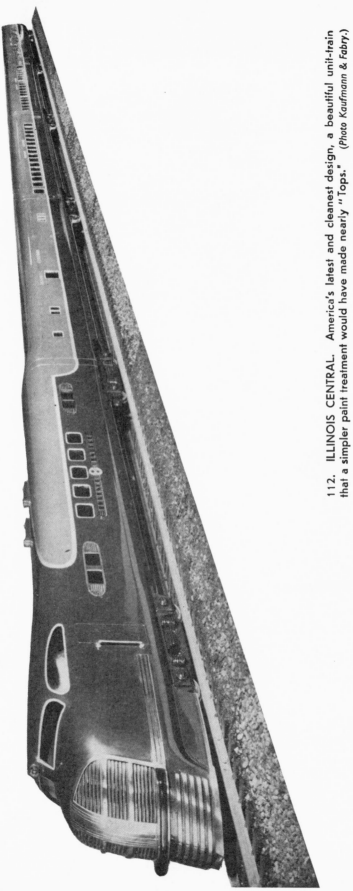

112. ILLINOIS CENTRAL. America's latest and cleanest design, a beautiful unit-train that a simpler paint treatment would have made nearly "Tops." *(Photo Kaufmann & Fabry.)*

Beautifully built by BUDD, here is the last word in
light alloy technique, being entirely made of shotweld
stainless steel.   But so far as appearance is concerned,
it is far from satisfactory.   Does not compare with the
NETHERLAND RAILWAYS unit. (*113. Ph. Zak-Lownsbery.*)

A glimpse of the future: the smooth, airfoil surface of BURLINGTON'S ZEPHYR. (114. Photo Dmitri.)

115   Smooth surface, clean lines, even the trucks are "faired in". Streamlining at its present best. *(Photo Ivan Dmitri)*

THE GOODYEAR ZEPPELIN COMET, an American streamlined unit-train with an uninviting front end. The interior, on the contrary, is really attractive. Too many rivets on the outer surface (but necessary on account of aluminium construction).

(116. Photo New York, New Haven and Hartford.)

THE GULF, MOBILE AND NORTHERN'S streamliner shows a decided improvement over similar designs. The decorations on the front end are unnecessarily complicating an otherwise pleasant body treatment. But still, it is no match to the Dutch train.

(117. Photo Gulf, Mobile and Northern Railway.)

118. Front and rear ends of the BURLINGTON ZEPHYR Diesel-electric unit trains. *(Photo Chicago, Burlington and Quincy Railroad.)*

America's most powerful Diesel-electric engine, greatly handicapped by a rather dreadful design treatment   The baroque camouflage is meant for visibility and acts as the "coup de grace" to a design already painful.   (119.   *Photo Atcheson, Topeka and Santa Fé.*)

SOVIET RUSSIA

SOVIET RUSSIA'S Deisel-electric engine, the most powerful in Europe and by all means the **most** unattractive. Like its neighbour across the page, this giant seems to have suffered at birth. A good example of bad design.

(120. *Photo Sovfoto.*)

AND FINALLY THE THREE
VITAL SAFETY FACTORS
THAT MAKE HIGHER
SPEEDS POSSIBLE : :

MAINTENANCE

Careful maintenance. Photograph taken in London and
North Eastern's locomotive shop. (121. Photo Hubschmann.)

SIGNALIZATION

Correct signalization is of paramount importance. In some countries it's a wonder that accidents are so scarce when one considers such a maze of steel. The signals themselves are submerged in the structural work, therefore thoroughly confusing. What a perfect field for simplification!

EENIE, MEENIE, MYNIE, MO—

(122 and 123.   *Photos Hubschmann.*)

BUT—more like Things to Come—
levers in electric signal box,
Brighton. SOUTHERN RAILWAY.

SWITCHING

Accurate switching is getting more and more complex. Slow freight trains must still be side-tracked in favour of extra fast passenger trains. A group of switch levers on the L.N.E.R. Neat and efficient. Inspires confidence. *(124. Photo Hubschmann.)*

SAFETY—point lock and electrical "watch-dog." The detector (with cover removed) proves the correct position of the points and the engagement of the bolt to the signalman before the signal can be operated. SOUTHERN RAILWAY. *(125. Photo Hübschmann.)*